CFO's Handbook to Cyber Security

2025 Edition

Chapter 1: Introduction

The Evolving Role of the CFO in Cybersecurity
The Chief Financial Officer (CFO) role has expanded beyond traditional financial management in the digital age. You must look at technology and cybersecurity, frequently leveraging outside resources to achieve this goal. Gone are the days when CFOs could solely focus on balancing the books and ensuring the organization's economic health. You are now at the forefront of cybersecurity efforts, safeguarding the organization's digital assets. CFOs are indeed the superheroes of the corporate realm! Equipped with sharp financial skills and dynamic spreadsheets, the modern CFO must look for cyber villains attacking from the shadows.

As organizations increasingly rely on technology to drive business operations, CFOs are now key players in ensuring their organizations' security. This chapter explores the evolving role of the CFO in cybersecurity, highlighting the importance of their involvement in protecting the organization's digital fortress. After all, who better to defend the kingdom than the one who holds the keys to the treasury?

Importance of Cybersecurity in 2025
Cybersecurity has become vital for businesses worldwide. Looking ahead to 2026, cyber threats are only becoming even more sophisticated and diverse. Organizations must adopt a proactive approach as cyber criminals continuously adapt their strategies, including leveraging AI to exploit potential vulnerabilities. This situation is analogous to a strategic game of cat and mouse, where both parties are constantly evolving. By prioritizing our defenses and working collaboratively, we can build a safer and more secure future for all.

This section delves into the significance of cybersecurity in 2025, emphasizing why CFOs must prioritize it as a key component of their strategic planning. With the rise of remote work, cloud computing, and the Internet of Things (IoT), the attack surface has expanded, providing cybercriminals with more opportunities to infiltrate systems. It's as if the digital world has become a giant playground for hackers, and CFOs are the vigilant playground monitors, ensuring everyone plays nice.

The CFO's Strategic Role
As strategic leaders, CFOs are uniquely positioned to drive cybersecurity initiatives. Their financial expertise allows them to allocate resources effectively, ensuring that cybersecurity measures are robust and cost-efficient. It's a delicate balancing act. But fear not; CFOs are becoming well-equipped to handle the challenge. Leveraging outside resources is often needed for a total cost of ownership savings.

This chapter discusses how CFOs can leverage their skills to develop comprehensive cybersecurity strategies that align with business objectives. By integrating cybersecurity into the overall business strategy, CFOs can ensure that security measures are not just an afterthought but a fundamental part of the organization's DNA. It's like adding a pinch of salt to a recipe – it might seem small, but it makes all the difference.

Collaboration with IT and Security Teams
Effective cybersecurity requires collaboration across various departments. CFOs must work closely with IT and security teams to implement and maintain security protocols. It's like assembling a superhero team; each member brings their unique skills to the table, and together, they can conquer any threat that comes their way. The villains' collective budget is estimated to be more than 20 trillion dollars in 2026, roughly the GDP of the entire European Union.

This section highlights the importance of cross-functional collaboration and provides insights into how CFOs can foster a culture of cybersecurity within their organizations. By breaking down silos and encouraging open communication, CFOs can ensure that everyone is on the same page when it comes to protecting the organization's digital assets. After all, teamwork makes the dream work – or, in this case, keeps the hackers at bay.

Building a Cybersecurity Culture
Creating a cybersecurity culture is essential for long-term success. CFOs play a crucial role in promoting awareness and education about cybersecurity risks. It's like being the wise elder in a village, imparting knowledge and wisdom to the younger generation. By fostering a

culture of vigilance and responsibility, CFOs can ensure that everyone in the organization understands the importance of cybersecurity.

This chapter outlines strategies for building a cybersecurity culture, including training programs, regular communication, and incentivizing best practices. By making cybersecurity a part of the organization's everyday life, CFOs can create an environment where security is second nature.

Conclusion

The introduction sets the stage for the rest of the book, emphasizing the critical role of CFOs in cybersecurity. As the digital landscape evolves, CFOs must adapt and take proactive measures to protect their organizations. This chapter serves as a foundation for understanding the importance of cybersecurity and the strategic role CFOs play in ensuring their organization's security.

In conclusion, the CFO's role in cybersecurity is no longer optional but necessary. By embracing their new responsibilities and working collaboratively with other departments, CFOs can become the unsung heroes of the digital age.

Chapter 2: Understanding Cyber Threats

Cyber threats have become a constant concern for organizations worldwide in the ever-evolving digital landscape. As technology advances, so do the tactics and strategies employed by cybercriminals. This chapter delves into the various types of cyber threats, emerging threats in 2025, and case studies of recent cyber attacks. By understanding the nature of these threats, CFOs can better prepare their organizations to defend against them.

Types of Cyber Threats
Cyber threats come in many forms, each with unique characteristics and potential impact. Here, we explore some of the most common types of cyber threats that organizations face today:

1. Malware: Malware, short for malicious software, is designed to infiltrate and damage computer systems. It includes viruses, worms, trojans, and ransomware. Imagine malware as the digital equivalent of a lousy houseguest who overstays their welcome and trashes the place.

2. Phishing: Phishing attacks involve tricking individuals into providing sensitive information by posing as trustworthy entities, such as login credentials or financial details. It's like receiving an email from a "Nigerian prince" who promises you a fortune in exchange for your bank account details. Spoiler alert: there is no prince, and your bank account will be emptied faster than you can say "cybersecurity."

3. Denial-of-Service (DoS) Attacks: DoS attacks aim to disrupt a website's or online service's normal functioning by overwhelming it with traffic. They're akin to a mob storming a store on Black Friday, causing chaos and preventing legitimate customers from entering.

4. Man-in-the-Middle (MitM) Attacks: In MitM attacks, cybercriminals intercept and alter communication between two parties without their knowledge. It's like having a nosy neighbor who listens to your conversations and spreads misinformation.

5. Advanced Persistent Threats (APTs): APTs are sophisticated, targeted attacks that involve prolonged efforts to infiltrate and remain undetected within a network. Think of APTs as stealthy ninjas who sneak into your organization and quietly gather intelligence over time.

Emerging Threats in 2025

As we move further into the digital age, new and emerging threats surface. In 2025, organizations must be vigilant against these evolving dangers:

1. AI-Powered Attacks: With the rise of artificial intelligence, cybercriminals are leveraging AI to enhance their attack strategies. AI-powered attacks can adapt and learn from defenses, making them more challenging to detect and counter. It's like facing an opponent who gets smarter with every move you make.

2. IoT Vulnerabilities: The Internet of Things (IoT) has brought convenience and connectivity to our lives but has also introduced new security risks. IoT devices, from smart thermostats to connected cars, can be exploited by cybercriminals to gain access to networks. It's as if every smart device in your home has the potential to become a spy.

3. Quantum Computing Threats: Quantum computing promises to revolutionize technology but poses a significant cybersecurity threat. Quantum computers can break encryption methods that are currently considered secure. It's like discovering that the lock on your front door can be picked with a paperclip.

4. Supply Chain Attacks: Cybercriminals increasingly target supply chains to infiltrate organizations. They can access the primary target by compromising a supplier or vendor. It's like sneaking into a castle by hiding in a delivery truck.

Case Studies of Recent Cyber Attacks

To illustrate the real-world impact of cyber threats, let's examine a few notable case studies of recent cyber attacks:

1. The SolarWinds Attack: In 2020, the SolarWinds attack made headlines as one of the most significant cyber espionage incidents in history. Cybercriminals infiltrated the software company's systems and used its Orion platform to distribute malware to numerous government and private sector organizations. The attack highlighted the vulnerability of supply chains and the importance of robust security measures.

2. The Colonial Pipeline Ransomware Attack: In 2021, the Colonial Pipeline ransomware attack disrupted fuel supplies across the eastern United States. Cybercriminals used ransomware to encrypt the company's data and demanded a ransom for its release. The incident underscored organizations' critical need for effective incident response plans and cybersecurity protocols.

3. The Equifax Data Breach: In 2017, Equifax experienced a massive data breach that exposed the personal information of over 147 million individuals. The breach was caused by a company's web application framework vulnerability. The Equifax case is a cautionary tale about the importance of regular security assessments and timely vulnerability patching.

Identifying and Assessing Cyber Risks

Understanding the types of cyber threats is just the first step. CFOs must also identify and assess cyber risks within their organizations. This involves evaluating the potential impact of various threats and determining the likelihood of their occurrence. CFOs can prioritize their cybersecurity efforts and allocate resources effectively by conducting thorough risk assessments.

Risk Mitigation Strategies

Once cyber risks have been identified and assessed, CFOs must implement mitigation strategies. This includes deploying security technologies, establishing policies and procedures, and fostering a culture of cybersecurity awareness. It's like building a fortress with multiple layers of defense – the more barriers you have, the harder it is for cybercriminals to breach.

Cyber Insurance: What CFOs Need to Know

In addition to traditional risk mitigation strategies, CFOs should consider cyber insurance as part of their cybersecurity plan. Cyber insurance can provide financial protection during a cyber incident, covering costs such as legal fees, data recovery, and business interruption. It's like having a safety net that cushions the blow when things go wrong.

Conclusion

Understanding cyber threats is crucial for CFOs as they navigate the complexities of modern financial leadership. By staying informed about the types of threats, emerging dangers, and real-world case studies, CFOs can better prepare their organizations to defend against cyber attacks. With the right strategies and a proactive approach, CFOs can become the guardians of their organization's digital assets, ensuring a secure and resilient future.

In conclusion, the digital landscape is fraught with challenges, but it also presents opportunities for CFOs to demonstrate their strategic leadership. By embracing their role in cybersecurity and working collaboratively with IT and security teams, CFOs can build a robust defense against cyber threats. So, don your armor and prepare for battle – the world of cybersecurity awaits.

Chapter 3: Cybersecurity Frameworks and Standards

In the ever-evolving world of cybersecurity, frameworks, and standards serve as the guiding principles that help organizations navigate the complex landscape of threats and vulnerabilities. These frameworks provide a structured approach to managing cybersecurity risks, ensuring compliance with regulatory requirements, and implementing best practices. This chapter will explore key cybersecurity frameworks, compliance and regulatory requirements, and how to implement cybersecurity best practices. And yes, we'll sprinkle in a bit of light professional humor to keep things engaging.

Overview of Key Frameworks

Cybersecurity frameworks are like the blueprints for building a secure digital fortress. They provide a systematic approach to identifying, assessing, and managing cybersecurity risks. Let's take a closer look at some of the most widely recognized frameworks:

1. NIST Cybersecurity Framework (CSF): The National Institute of Standards and Technology (NIST) Cybersecurity Framework is a comprehensive guide designed to help organizations manage and reduce cybersecurity risks. It consists of five core functions: Identify, Protect, Detect, Respond, and Recover. Think of it as the Swiss Army knife of cybersecurity frameworks – versatile, reliable, and essential for any organization.

2. ISO/IEC 27001: The International Organization for Standardization (ISO) and the International Electrotechnical Commission (IEC) developed ISO/IEC 27001, a standard for information security management systems (ISMS). This framework systematically manages sensitive company information, ensuring its confidentiality, integrity, and availability. It's like having a well-organized filing cabinet where everything is in its place and securely locked away.

3. CIS Controls: The Center for Internet Security (CIS) Controls is a set of best practices for securing IT systems and data. It consists of 20 critical security controls that organizations can implement to protect against cyber threats. Think of the CIS Controls as a checklist for cybersecurity hygiene – follow it, and you'll be in good shape.

4. COBIT: Control Objectives for Information and Related Technologies (COBIT) is an IT governance and management framework. It provides a comprehensive approach to aligning IT with business goals, ensuring that IT investments deliver value and mitigate risks. COBIT is like the project manager of cybersecurity frameworks, keeping everything on track and ensuring that nothing falls through the cracks.

Compliance and Regulatory Requirements

In addition to following cybersecurity frameworks, organizations must comply with various regulatory requirements. These regulations protect sensitive information and ensure that organizations appropriately safeguard their data. Here are some key regulatory requirements that CFOs should be aware of:

1. General Data Protection Regulation (GDPR): The GDPR is a European Union regulation that governs the processing of personal data. It imposes strict requirements on organizations to protect the privacy and rights of individuals. Non-compliance can result in hefty fines, so taking GDPR seriously is essential. Think of it as the digital equivalent of a stern school principal – you don't want to get on its bad side.

2. Health Insurance Portability and Accountability Act (HIPAA): This U.S. regulation sets standards for protecting sensitive patient information. It requires healthcare organizations to implement safeguards to ensure the confidentiality, integrity, and availability of electronic protected health information (ePHI). HIPAA is like the health inspector of the digital world. It makes sure that everything is clean and secure.

3. Sarbanes-Oxley Act (SOX): SOX is a U.S. regulation that aims to protect investors by improving the accuracy and reliability of corporate disclosures. It requires organizations to implement internal controls and procedures for financial reporting. SOX is like a financial watchdog, keeping an eye on everything to ensure transparency and accountability.

4. Payment Card Industry Data Security Standard (PCI DSS): PCI DSS is a set of security standards designed to protect cardholder data. It applies to organizations that handle credit card transactions and requires them to implement specific security measures. PCI DSS is like the bouncer at a nightclub, ensuring that only authorized individuals get in and everyone inside is safe.

Implementing Cybersecurity Best Practices

Now that we've covered the key frameworks and regulatory requirements let's dive into how organizations can implement cybersecurity best practices. These best practices are like the secret sauce that makes everything work together seamlessly. Here are some essential steps to get started:

1. Conduct a Risk Assessment: The first step in implementing cybersecurity best practices is conducting a thorough risk assessment. This involves identifying potential threats, assessing their likelihood and impact, and determining the organization's risk tolerance. It's like taking a hard look at your digital landscape and figuring out where the weak spots are.

2. Develop a Cybersecurity Policy: A cybersecurity policy is a formal document that outlines the organization's approach to managing cybersecurity risks. It should include guidelines for acceptable use, data protection, incident response, and employee training. Think of it as the rulebook for your digital fortress – everyone needs to know the rules to keep things secure.

3. Implement Security Controls: Organizations should implement appropriate security controls based on the risk assessment and cybersecurity policy. This includes technical controls (e.g., firewalls, encryption), administrative controls (e.g., access controls, security awareness training), and physical controls (e.g., secure facilities, surveillance). It's like building layers of defense – the more layers you have, the harder it is for cybercriminals to break through.

4. Monitor and Review: Cybersecurity is not a one-time effort – it's an ongoing process. Organizations should continuously monitor their systems for potential threats and regularly review their security controls to ensure they remain effective. It's like tending to a garden – you need to keep an eye on things and make adjustments to keep everything healthy and thriving.

5. Incident Response Planning: Cyber incidents can still occur despite the best efforts. That's why it's essential to have an incident response plan in place. This plan should outline the steps to take in the event of a cyber incident, including how to contain the threat, mitigate damage, and recover. Think of it as your digital fire drill; everyone must know what to do when things go wrong.

6. Employee Training and Awareness: Employees are often the first line of defense against cyber threats. Organizations should invest in regular cybersecurity training and awareness programs to ensure employees understand the risks and how to protect themselves and the organization. It's like teaching everyone in the castle how to defend against invaders – the more prepared they are, the better.

Conclusion

Cybersecurity frameworks and standards provide a structured approach to managing cybersecurity risks and ensuring compliance with regulatory requirements. Organizations can build a robust defense against cyber threats by following these frameworks and implementing best practices. CFOs play a crucial role in this process, leveraging their financial expertise to allocate resources effectively and ensure that cybersecurity measures are robust and cost-efficient.

In conclusion, navigating the complex cybersecurity landscape requires strategic planning, collaboration, and continuous improvement. By embracing their role in cybersecurity and working closely with IT and security teams, CFOs can help their organizations stay ahead of the curve and protect their digital assets. So, wear your cybersecurity hat and prepare to lead your organization to a secure and resilient future.

Chapter 4: Risk Management and Assessment

In cybersecurity, risk management and assessment are like the bread and butter of a well-rounded security strategy. Without them, you're essentially flying blind, hoping that cyber threats will pass you by. Spoiler alert: they won't. This chapter delves into the nitty-gritty of identifying and assessing cyber risks, implementing risk mitigation strategies, and understanding the role of cyber insurance. And yes, we'll keep things light with a touch of professional humor to make the journey more enjoyable.

Identifying and Assessing Cyber Risks

The first step in managing cyber risks is to identify and assess them. This process involves understanding the potential threats to your organization, evaluating their likelihood and impact, and determining your organization's risk tolerance. Think of it as a digital version of a health check-up. You need to know what's wrong before fixing it.

1. Identifying Cyber Risks: Cyber risks come in many shapes and sizes, from malware and phishing attacks to insider threats and data breaches. To identify these risks, organizations should thoroughly inventory their digital assets, including hardware, software, data, and network infrastructure. It's like taking stock of everything in your digital kingdom. You need to know what you have to protect it effectively.

2. Assessing Likelihood and Impact: Once you've identified potential risks, the next step is to assess their likelihood and impact. This involves evaluating how likely a particular threat will occur and the possible damage it could cause. It's like playing a game of "what if" … what if a hacker gains access to your customer database? What if a ransomware attack locks you out of your systems? By considering these scenarios, you can prioritize your cybersecurity efforts.

3. Determining Risk Tolerance: Every organization has a different level of risk tolerance, depending on factors such as industry, size, and regulatory requirements. Risk tolerance is the amount of risk an organization is willing to accept to pursue its objectives. It's like deciding how much spice you can handle in your food – some people like it mild, while others prefer it extra hot.

Risk Mitigation Strategies

Once you've identified and assessed your cyber risks, the next step is implementing mitigation strategies. Risk mitigation involves reducing the likelihood and impact of cyber threats. Here are some common risk mitigation strategies:

1. Implementing Security Controls: Security controls are measures designed to protect your digital assets from cyber threats. These controls can be technical (e.g., firewalls, encryption), administrative (e.g., access controls, security policies), or physical (e.g., secure facilities, surveillance). Think of security controls as your digital fortress's locks, alarms, and guard dogs. They keep the bad guys out and the good stuff in.

2. Regular Security Assessments: Regular security assessments are essential for identifying vulnerabilities and ensuring adequate security controls. These can include vulnerability scans, penetration testing, and security audits. It's like getting a regular check-up at the doctor. You need to catch any issues early before they become serious problems.

3. Employee Training and Awareness: Employees are often the first line of defense against cyber threats. Regular cybersecurity training and awareness programs can help employees recognize and respond to potential threats. It's like teaching everyone in your organization to be a digital bodyguard – the more they know, the better they can protect themselves and the organization.

4. Incident Response Planning: Cyber incidents can still occur despite your best efforts. An incident response plan ensures you can respond quickly and effectively to minimize damage. This plan should outline the steps to take in the event of a cyber incident, including how to contain the threat, mitigate damage, and recover. Think of it as your digital fire drill. Everyone needs to know what to do when things go wrong.

Cyber Insurance: What CFOs Need to Know

In addition to traditional risk mitigation strategies, cyber insurance can provide your organization with an extra layer of protection. Cyber insurance is designed to cover the financial costs of cyber incidents, such as legal fees, data recovery, and business interruption. It's like having a safety net that cushions the blow when things go wrong.

1. Understanding Cyber Insurance Coverage: Cyber insurance policies can vary widely regarding coverage and exclusions. It's essential to understand what your policy covers and what it doesn't. Common coverage areas include data breaches, ransomware attacks, business interruption, and legal expenses. It's like reading the fine print on a warranty – you need to know what's included and what's not.

2. Choosing the Right Policy: Selecting the right cyber insurance policy involves evaluating your organization's needs and risk profile. Consider factors such as your organization's size, the nature of your digital assets, and your risk tolerance. It's like shopping for a new car; you must find the one that fits your needs and budget.

3. Working with Insurers: Building a good relationship with your cyber insurance provider can help you get the most out of your policy. This includes providing accurate information about your organization's cybersecurity measures and promptly reporting any incidents. It's like having a good relationship with your mechanic – the better they know your car, the better they can help you when something goes wrong.

Building a Cybersecurity Culture

Creating a cybersecurity culture is essential for long-term success. A strong cybersecurity culture ensures that everyone in the organization understands the importance of cybersecurity and takes responsibility for protecting digital assets. Here are some strategies for building a cybersecurity culture:

1. Leadership Commitment: Leadership commitment is crucial for fostering a cybersecurity culture. When leaders prioritize cybersecurity and lead by example, it sends a clear message to the rest of the organization. It's like having a captain who steers the ship – everyone follows their lead.

2. Regular Communication: Regular communication about cybersecurity risks and best practices helps employees remember cybersecurity. This can include newsletters, training sessions, and security alerts. It's like keeping everyone in the loop. The more informed they are, the better they can protect themselves and the organization.

3. Incentivizing Best Practices: Incentivizing employees to follow cybersecurity best practices can help reinforce positive behavior. This can include rewards for completing training programs, recognizing employees who identify potential threats, and incorporating cybersecurity into performance evaluations. It's like giving a gold star for good behavior – encouraging everyone to do their best.

4. Creating a Supportive Environment: Building a cybersecurity culture requires creating a supportive environment where employees feel comfortable reporting potential threats and asking questions. This includes providing clear channels for reporting incidents and offering support and resources for employees. It's like having an open-door policy. The more approachable you are, the more employees will likely come to you with concerns.

Conclusion

Risk management and assessment are critical components of a robust cybersecurity strategy. By identifying and assessing cyber risks, implementing risk mitigation strategies, and understanding the role of cyber insurance, CFOs can help their organizations build a strong defense against cyber threats. Building a cybersecurity culture further reinforces these efforts, ensuring that everyone in the organization takes responsibility for protecting digital assets.

In conclusion, managing cyber risks is an ongoing process that requires vigilance, collaboration, and continuous improvement. By embracing their role in cybersecurity and working closely with IT and security teams, CFOs can help their organizations stay ahead of the curve and protect their digital assets. So, wear your risk management hat and prepare to lead your organization to a secure and resilient future.

Chapter 5: Building a Cybersecurity Strategy

In cybersecurity, having a well-defined strategy is akin to having a roadmap for navigating a treacherous terrain. Without it, you'll likely find yourself lost, vulnerable, and at the mercy of cyber threats. This chapter delves into the essentials of building a comprehensive cybersecurity strategy, aligning it with business objectives, budgeting for cybersecurity, and ensuring that your organization is prepared for the digital challenges of 2025. And, of course, we'll keep things engaging with a touch of light professional humor.

Developing a Comprehensive Cybersecurity Plan

Creating a cybersecurity plan is like preparing for a grand adventure. You need to know where you're going, what obstacles you might encounter, and how to overcome them. A comprehensive cybersecurity plan should include the following key elements:

1. Risk Assessment: A thorough risk assessment is the foundation of any cybersecurity plan. This involves identifying potential threats, assessing their likelihood and impact, and determining your organization's risk tolerance. Think of it as scouting the terrain before embarking on your journey – you need to know where the pitfalls are to avoid them.

2. Security Controls: Based on the risk assessment, you must implement appropriate security controls to protect your digital assets. These controls can be technical (e.g., firewalls, encryption), administrative (e.g., access controls, security policies), or physical (e.g., secure facilities, surveillance). It's like packing the right gear for your adventure – the more prepared you are, the better.

3. Incident Response Plan: Cyber incidents can still occur despite your best efforts. An incident response plan ensures you can respond quickly and effectively to minimize damage. This plan should outline the steps to take in the event of a cyber incident, including how to contain the threat, mitigate damage, and recover. Think of it as your emergency kit – you must know what to do when things go wrong.

4. Employee Training and Awareness: Employees are often the first line of defense against cyber threats. Regular cybersecurity training and awareness programs can help employees recognize and respond to potential threats. It's like teaching everyone in your organization to be a digital bodyguard – the more they know, the better they can protect themselves and the organization.

5. Continuous Monitoring and Improvement: Cybersecurity is not a one-time effort – it's an ongoing process. Organizations should continuously monitor their systems for potential threats and regularly review their security controls to ensure they remain effective. It's like watching the weather during your adventure – you must be prepared for changes.

Aligning Cybersecurity with Business Objectives

A successful cybersecurity strategy should align with your organization's business objectives. This means integrating cybersecurity into the overall business strategy and ensuring security measures support the organization's goals. Here are some key considerations for aligning cybersecurity with business objectives:

1. Understanding Business Goals: The first step in aligning cybersecurity with business objectives is understanding the organization's goals and priorities. This includes identifying key business processes, critical assets, and strategic initiatives. It's like knowing the destination of your adventure – you need to know where you're headed to plan your route.

2. Risk Management: Effective risk management involves balancing the need for security with the organization's risk tolerance and business objectives. This means prioritizing cybersecurity efforts based on their potential impact on the organization's goals. It's like deciding which obstacles to tackle first; you need to focus on the ones that pose the greatest threat to your journey.

3. Collaboration with Stakeholders: Collaboration with stakeholders is essential for aligning cybersecurity with business objectives. This includes working with IT, security, and business teams to ensure security measures support the organization's goals. It's like assembling a team for your adventure – everyone must work together to succeed.

4. Communication and Reporting: Regular communication and reporting about cybersecurity efforts help keep stakeholders informed and engaged. This includes providing updates on security initiatives, risk assessments, and incident response activities. It's like keeping everyone in the loop during your adventure – the more informed they are, the better they can support your efforts.

Budgeting for Cybersecurity

Budgeting for cybersecurity is a critical aspect of building a comprehensive strategy. It involves allocating resources effectively to ensure that security measures are robust and cost-efficient. Here are some key considerations for budgeting for cybersecurity:

1. Assessing Costs: The first step in budgeting for cybersecurity is to assess the costs associated with implementing security measures. This includes hardware, software, personnel, training, and incident response costs. It's like calculating the expenses for your adventure – you need to know how much it will cost to be prepared.

2. Prioritizing Investments: Based on the risk assessment and business objectives, you'll need to prioritize your cybersecurity investments. This means focusing on the areas that pose the most significant risk and significantly impact the organization's goals. It's like deciding which gear to invest in for your adventure – you must focus on the essentials.

3. Allocating Resources: Effective resource allocation involves distributing the budget across various cybersecurity initiatives. This includes funding for security controls, employee training, incident response, and continuous monitoring. It's like packing your gear for the adventure – you must ensure you have everything you need.

4. Monitoring and Adjusting: Budgeting for cybersecurity is an ongoing process that requires regular monitoring and adjustments. This includes reviewing the effectiveness of security measures and reallocating resources as needed. It's like watching your expenses during the adventure – you must stay within budget.

Preparing for the Digital Challenges of 2025

As we move further into the digital age, organizations must be prepared for the evolving challenges of cybersecurity in 2025. This includes staying informed about emerging threats, adopting new technologies, and continuously improving security measures. Here are some key considerations for preparing for the digital challenges of 2025:

1. Staying Informed: Staying informed about emerging threats and trends is essential for preparing for the digital challenges of 2025. This includes monitoring industry reports, attending conferences, and participating in cybersecurity forums. It's like watching the horizon during your adventure – you must know what's coming.

2. Adopting New Technologies: Adopting new technologies can help organizations stay ahead of the curve and enhance their cybersecurity efforts. This includes leveraging artificial intelligence, machine learning, and automation to improve security measures. It's like upgrading your gear for the adventure – the better equipped you are, the more successful you'll be.

3. Continuous Improvement: Continuous improvement involves regularly reviewing and updating security measures to ensure they remain effective. This includes conducting security assessments, implementing new controls, and providing ongoing training. It's like refining your skills during an adventure—the more you practice, the better you'll become.

4. Building Resilience: Building resilience involves preparing for the unexpected and ensuring your organization can recover quickly from cyber incidents. This includes developing robust incident response plans, investing in cyber insurance, and fostering a culture of cybersecurity awareness. It's like having a backup plan for your adventure – you must be prepared for surprises.

Conclusion

Building a comprehensive cybersecurity strategy is essential for navigating the digital challenges of 2025. By developing a well-defined plan, aligning it with business objectives, budgeting effectively, and preparing for emerging threats, CFOs can help their organizations build a robust defense against cyber threats. Collaboration with stakeholders and continuous improvement further reinforce these efforts, ensuring that security measures remain effective and support the organization's goals.

In conclusion, a successful cybersecurity strategy requires strategic planning, resource allocation, and ongoing vigilance. By embracing their role in cybersecurity and working closely with IT and security teams, CFOs can lead their organizations to a secure and resilient future. So, put on your cybersecurity hat and prepare to build a robust cybersecurity strategy.

Chapter 6: Technology and Tools

In the ever-evolving landscape of cybersecurity, technology, and tools play a crucial role in protecting organizations from cyber threats. This chapter explores the various tools and strategies CFOs can use to enhance their cybersecurity efforts, from essential cybersecurity technologies to leveraging AI and automation. We'll also delve into choosing a Managed Service Provider (MSP) to work with, ensuring that your organization is well-equipped to tackle the digital challenges of 2025. And, as always, we'll keep things engaging with a touch of light professional humor.

Essential Cybersecurity Technologies

Regarding cybersecurity, having the right technologies in place is like having a well-stocked toolbox – you need the right tools for the job. Here are some essential cybersecurity technologies that every organization should consider:

1. Firewalls: Firewalls act as the first line of defense against cyber threats by monitoring and controlling incoming and outgoing network traffic. Think of firewalls as the digital equivalent of a security guard at the entrance of your building – they keep the bad guys out and let the good guys in.

2. Intrusion Detection Systems (IDS): IDS are designed to detect and respond to suspicious activities within a network. They monitor network traffic for signs of potential threats and alert administrators when something fishy happens. It's like having a watchdog that barks when it senses danger – you want to know when something's amiss.

3. Antivirus Software: Antivirus software is essential for protecting against malware and other malicious software. It scans files and programs for known threats and removes them before they can cause harm. Think of antivirus software as the digital equivalent of a flu shot – it helps prevent infections and keeps your systems healthy.

4. Encryption: Encryption converts data into a secure format that can only be accessed by authorized individuals. It ensures that sensitive information remains confidential and protected from unauthorized access. It's like putting your valuables in a safe—only those with the key can access them.

5. Multi-Factor Authentication (MFA): MFA adds an extra layer of security by requiring users to provide multiple verification forms before accessing systems or data. These forms can include something they know (e.g., a password), something they have (e.g., a smartphone), or something they are (e.g., a fingerprint). Think of MFA as the digital equivalent of a double-lock system; it's much harder to break in.

Leveraging AI and Automation in Cybersecurity

Artificial intelligence (AI) and automation are transforming the cybersecurity landscape by enhancing the ability to detect and respond to threats. Here are some ways that AI and automation can be leveraged in cybersecurity:

1. Threat Detection: AI-powered threat detection systems can analyze vast amounts of data to identify patterns and anomalies that may indicate a cyber threat. These systems can adapt and learn from new threats, making them more effective. It's like having a super-smart detective on your team – they can spot clues that others might miss.

2. Incident Response: Automation can streamline the incident response process by automatically executing predefined actions when a threat is detected. These include isolating affected systems, notifying administrators, and initiating recovery procedures. Consider automation your digital first responder—it quickly contains the threat and minimizes damage.

3. Predictive Analytics: AI can predict potential threats based on historical data and trends. By analyzing past incidents, AI can identify patterns and forecast future risks, allowing organizations to take proactive measures. It's like having a crystal ball that helps you see into the future; you can prepare for what's coming.

4. Security Orchestration: Security orchestration platforms use automation to coordinate and manage security tools and processes. They integrate various technologies and streamline workflows, making it easier to manage cybersecurity efforts. Think of security orchestration as an orchestra conductor – they ensure that all the instruments play harmoniously.

Evaluating and Selecting Cybersecurity Vendors

Choosing the right cybersecurity vendors is essential for building a robust defense against cyber threats. Here are some key considerations for evaluating and selecting cybersecurity vendors:

1. Assessing Vendor Capabilities: The first step in selecting a cybersecurity vendor is to assess their capabilities. This includes evaluating their products and services, expertise, and track record. It's like interviewing candidates for a job – you want to know what they bring.

2. Understanding Vendor Reputation: Reputation matters when it comes to cybersecurity vendors. Look for vendors with a strong reputation for reliability, customer service, and innovation. It's like checking reviews before buying a product – you want to know what others think.

3. Evaluating Cost and Value: Cost is an essential but not the only consideration. Evaluate the vendor's value in terms of features, support, and overall effectiveness. It's like comparing the price and quality of different products; you want the best bang for your buck.

4. Ensuring Compatibility: Ensure the vendor's products and services are compatible with your existing systems and infrastructure. This includes checking for integration capabilities and ease of deployment. It's like ensuring that new furniture fits your living room – you want everything to work together seamlessly.

Choosing a Managed Service Provider (MSP)

Working with a Managed Service Provider (MSP) can be a game-changer for organizations looking to enhance their cybersecurity efforts. MSPs provide various services, from monitoring and managing security systems to responding to incidents and providing expert guidance. Here are some key considerations for choosing an MSP:

1. Understanding MSP Services: The first step in choosing an MSP is understanding its services. These include network monitoring, threat detection, incident response, and security consulting. It's like reading the menu at a restaurant—you want to know what's available.

2. Evaluating MSP Expertise: Expertise is crucial for MSPs. Look for providers with a proven track record in cybersecurity and a team of experienced professionals. It's like hiring a skilled chef – you want someone who knows their stuff.

3. Assessing MSP Reliability: Reliability is essential for MSPs, as you'll be entrusting them with the security of your digital assets. Look for providers with a strong reputation for reliability and customer service. It's like choosing a dependable car – you want something that won't break down.

4. Considering MSP Cost: Cost is an essential but not the only consideration. Evaluate the MSP's value regarding services, support, and overall effectiveness. It's like comparing the price and quality of different dishes – you want the best value for your money.

5. Ensuring MSP Compatibility: Ensure the MSP's services are compatible with your existing systems and infrastructure. This includes checking for integration capabilities and ease of deployment. It's like ensuring new ingredients work well in your recipe – you want everything to blend seamlessly.

Conclusion

Technology and tools are essential components of a robust cybersecurity strategy. From essential cybersecurity technologies to leveraging AI and automation, organizations have various options to enhance their security efforts. Choosing the right cybersecurity vendors and working with an MSP can further strengthen your defenses, ensuring that your organization is well-equipped to tackle the digital challenges of 2025.

In conclusion, building a strong cybersecurity strategy requires a combination of the right technologies, expert guidance, and continuous improvement. By embracing their role in cybersecurity and working closely with IT and security teams, CFOs can lead their organizations to a secure and resilient future. So, put on your cybersecurity hat and get ready to explore the world of technology and tools – the digital challenges of 2025 await.

Chapter 7: Working with Managed Service Providers (MSPs)

In the ever-evolving cybersecurity landscape, Managed Service Providers (MSPs) have become invaluable allies for organizations looking to bolster their defenses against cyber threats. MSPs offer various services, from monitoring and managing security systems to responding to incidents and providing expert guidance. This chapter delves into the essentials of working with MSPs, including selecting the right provider, understanding their services, and fostering a successful partnership. And, of course, we'll keep things engaging with a touch of light professional humor.

The Role of MSPs in Cybersecurity

Managed Service Providers (MSPs) are crucial in helping organizations manage their cybersecurity efforts. By outsourcing certain security functions to MSPs, organizations can leverage the expertise and resources of these providers to enhance their overall security posture. Think of MSPs as the trusty sidekicks to your cybersecurity superhero team – they bring specialized skills and tools to the table, allowing you to focus on your core business activities.

MSPs offer a wide range of services, including:

- **Network Monitoring:** MSPs continuously monitor your network for signs of suspicious activity, ensuring that potential threats are detected and addressed promptly. It's like having a vigilant night watchman who never sleeps.

- **Threat Detection and Response:** MSPs use advanced tools and techniques to detect and respond to cyber threats in real time. They can quickly identify and mitigate threats, minimizing the impact on your organization. Think of them as the digital firefighters rushing in to extinguish flames.

- **Security Assessments:** MSPs conduct regular security assessments to identify vulnerabilities and recommend improvements. This includes vulnerability scans, penetration testing, and security audits. It's like having a health check-up for your digital infrastructure – you must catch any issues early before they become serious problems.

- **Incident Response:** In the event of a cyber incident, MSPs provide expert guidance and support to help you respond effectively. They can assist with containment, eradication, and recovery efforts, ensuring that your organization gets back on its feet quickly. Think of them as the emergency response team that springs into action when disaster strikes.

- **Compliance and Regulatory Support:** MSPs help organizations navigate the complex landscape of cybersecurity regulations and compliance requirements. They can assist with meeting standards such as GDPR, HIPAA, and PCI DSS, ensuring your organization stays on the right side of the law. It's like having a legal advisor who keeps you out of trouble.

Selecting the Right MSP

Choosing the right MSP is a critical decision that can significantly impact your organization's cybersecurity efforts. Here are some key considerations for selecting the right MSP:

1. Assessing MSP Capabilities: The first step in selecting an MSP is to assess its capabilities. This includes evaluating its products and services, expertise, and track record. It's like interviewing candidates for a job—you want to know what they bring to the table. Look for MSPs with a proven track record in cybersecurity and a team of experienced professionals. Ask about their certifications, industry experience, and the technologies they use.

2. Understanding MSP Services: It's essential to understand the MSP's services and how they align with your organization's needs. This includes network monitoring, threat detection, incident response, and compliance support. Think of it as reading the menu at a restaurant – you want to know what's available and how it fits your requirements. Ensure the MSP offers a comprehensive suite of services covering all aspects of cybersecurity.

3. Evaluating Cost and Value: Cost is an essential factor but not the only consideration. Evaluate the MSP's value in terms of features, support, and overall effectiveness. It's like comparing the price and quality of different products – you want the best bang for your buck. Consider the total cost of ownership, including any hidden fees or additional charges. Look for MSPs that offer flexible pricing models and scalable solutions that can grow with your organization.

4. Ensuring Compatibility: Ensure the MSP's services are compatible with your existing systems and infrastructure. This includes checking for integration capabilities and ease of deployment. It's like ensuring that new furniture fits your living room – you want everything to work together seamlessly. Ask about the MSP's experience with your specific industry and technology stack. Ensure they integrate with your existing tools and processes without causing disruptions.

5. Checking References and Reviews: Before deciding, check references and reviews from other organizations that have worked with the MSP. This can provide valuable insights into their performance and reliability. It's like reading reviews before buying a product – you want to know what others think. Look for testimonials, case studies, and independent reviews to understand the MSP's reputation and customer satisfaction.

Fostering a Successful Partnership

Once you've selected the right MSP, fostering a successful partnership is essential for maximizing the benefits of their services. Here are some key strategies for building a strong relationship with your MSP:

1. Clear Communication: Clear and open communication is the foundation of a successful partnership. Establish regular communication channels and set expectations for reporting and updates. It's like having a good conversation with a friend – you must keep each other informed. Schedule regular meetings to discuss performance, review incidents, and plan for future improvements. Please make sure both parties understand their roles and responsibilities.

2. Setting Goals and Objectives: Work with your MSP to set clear goals and objectives for your cybersecurity efforts. This includes defining key performance indicators (KPIs) and metrics for success. Think of it as setting the destination for your journey – you need to know where you're headed to plan your route. Align your goals with your organization's overall business objectives and ensure the MSP understands your priorities.

3. Collaboration and Teamwork: Collaboration and teamwork are essential for a successful partnership. Work closely with your MSP to implement security measures, respond to incidents, and continuously improve your cybersecurity posture. It's like playing on a sports team – everyone must work together to succeed. Foster a culture of collaboration and trust and encourage open communication and feedback.

4. Continuous Improvement: Cybersecurity is an ongoing process that requires continuous improvement. Work with your MSP to regularly review and update your security measures, conduct security assessments, and implement new controls. It's like refining your skills during your adventure – the more you practice, the better you'll become. Stay informed about emerging threats and trends, and proactively address potential risks.

5. Building Trust: Trust is essential for a successful partnership. Trust your MSP to provide expert guidance and support and be transparent about your organization's needs and challenges. It's like building a strong foundation for a house; trust is the cornerstone of a successful relationship. Be open and honest in your communications and work together to address any issues or concerns.

Leveraging MSP Expertise

One of the key benefits of working with an MSP is leveraging their expertise to enhance your cybersecurity efforts. Here are some ways to make the most of your MSP's expertise:

1. Access to Specialized Skills: MSPs bring specialized skills and knowledge to the table, allowing you to benefit from their expertise without hiring additional staff. It's like having a team of experts on call – you can tap into their knowledge whenever needed. Use their experience and insights to address complex security challenges and implement best practices.

2. Staying Informed: MSPs stay up-to-date with cybersecurity trends, threats, and technologies. They can provide valuable insights and recommendations to help you stay ahead of the curve. It's like having a personal advisor who informs you about the latest developments. Regularly consult your MSP to stay informed about emerging threats and new security technologies.

3. Enhancing Incident Response: MSPs can enhance incident response capabilities by providing expert guidance and support during cyber incidents. They can help you respond quickly and effectively, minimizing damage and ensuring a swift recovery. Think of them as digital first responders – they quickly contain the threat and mitigate damage. Work with your MSP to develop and refine your incident response plan and conduct regular drills to ensure readiness.

4. Improving Compliance: MSPs can help you navigate the complex landscape of cybersecurity regulations and compliance requirements. They can assist with meeting standards such as GDPR, HIPAA, and PCI DSS, ensuring that your organization stays compliant. It's like having a legal advisor who keeps you out of trouble. Leverage their expertise to develop and implement compliance strategies and stay informed about regulatory changes.

5. Optimizing Security Investments: MSPs can help you optimize your security investments by providing insights into the most effective and cost-efficient security measures. They can recommend technologies and solutions that align with your organization's needs and budget. It's like having a financial advisor who helps you make smart investments. Work with your MSP to develop a cybersecurity budget and prioritize investments based on risk and impact.

Conclusion

Working with Managed Service Providers (MSPs) can significantly enhance your organization's cybersecurity efforts. By selecting the right MSP, fostering a successful partnership, and leveraging their expertise, you can build a robust defense against cyber threats. Clear communication, collaboration, and continuous improvement are essential for maximizing the benefits of your MSP partnership.

In conclusion, Managed Service Providers (MSPs) are invaluable allies in the fight against cyber threats. By embracing their role in cybersecurity and working closely with your MSP, you can lead your organization to a secure and resilient future. So, put on your cybersecurity hat and get ready to build a strong partnership with your MSP – the digital challenges of 2025 await.

Chapter 8: Incident Response and Recovery

In the world of cybersecurity, incidents are bound to happen. It's not a matter of if but when. That's why having a robust incident response and recovery plan is essential for any organization. This chapter delves into the essentials of preparing for cyber incidents, executing an effective incident response plan, and recovering from cyber incidents. We'll also explore lessons learned from past incidents to help you build a resilient cybersecurity strategy. And, of course, we'll keep things engaging with a touch of light professional humor.

Preparing for Cyber Incidents

Preparation is key when it comes to incident response. The more prepared you are, the better you'll be able to handle a cyber incident when it occurs. Here are some essential steps for preparing for cyber incidents:

1. Risk Assessment: A thorough risk assessment is the foundation of any incident response plan. This involves identifying potential threats, assessing their likelihood and impact, and determining your organization's risk tolerance. Think of it as scouting the terrain before embarking on your journey – you need to know where the pitfalls are to avoid them.

2. Incident Response Team: Establishing an incident response team is crucial for effective incident response. This team should include representatives from IT, security, legal, communications, and other relevant departments. It's like assembling a superhero team – each member brings their unique skills to the table, and together, they can conquer any threat that comes their way.

3. Incident Response Plan: A comprehensive incident response plan guides your organization's response to cyber incidents. This plan should outline the steps to take in the event of a cyber incident, including how to contain the threat, mitigate damage, and recover. Think of it as your emergency kit – you must know what to do when things go wrong.

4. Employee Training and Awareness: Employees are often the first line of defense against cyber threats. Regular cybersecurity training and awareness programs can help employees recognize and respond to potential threats. It's like teaching everyone in your organization to be a digital bodyguard – the more they know, the better they can protect themselves and the organization.

5. Continuous Monitoring: Continuous monitoring of your systems is essential for detecting potential threats and responding quickly to incidents. This includes using tools such as intrusion detection systems (IDS), security information and event management (SIEM) systems, and network monitoring tools. It's like watching the weather during your adventure – you must be prepared for changes.

Executing an Effective Incident Response Plan

When a cyber incident occurs, executing an effective incident response plan is crucial for minimizing damage and recovering quickly. Here are some key steps for implementing an incident response plan:

1. Detection and Identification: The first step in responding to a cyber incident is detecting and identifying the threat. This involves monitoring your systems for signs of suspicious activity and using tools such as IDS and SIEM systems to identify potential threats. It's like spotting a storm on the horizon – you must know what's coming to prepare for it.

2. Containment: Once the threat has been identified, the next step is to contain it. This involves isolating affected systems, blocking malicious traffic, and preventing the threat from spreading. Think of it as putting up sandbags to protect your home from flooding – you need to contain the danger to minimize damage.

3. Eradication: After the threat has been contained, the next step is to eradicate it. This involves removing malicious software, closing vulnerabilities, and eliminating the threat. It's like cleaning up after a storm – you must ensure everything is back to normal.

4. Recovery: Once the threat has been eradicated, the next step is to recover. This involves restoring affected systems, recovering lost data, and ensuring your organization returns to normal operations. Think of it as rebuilding after a storm – you must get everything back in order.

5. Communication: Effective communication is essential during a cyber incident. This includes notifying affected parties, providing updates to stakeholders, and coordinating with external partners such as law enforcement and regulatory agencies. It's like keeping everyone in the loop during a crisis – the more informed they are, the better they can support your efforts.

Post-Incident Recovery and Lessons Learned

Recovering from a cyber incident is not just about returning to normal operations – it's also about learning from the experience and improving your cybersecurity strategy. Here are some key steps for post-incident recovery and lessons learned:

1. Post-Incident Review: Conducting a post-incident review is essential for understanding what happened, how it was handled, and what can be improved. This involves analyzing the incident, reviewing the response, and identifying areas for improvement. It's like debriefing after a mission – you need to know what went well and what didn't to improve for next time.

2. Updating the Incident Response Plan: Based on the post-incident review, update your incident response plan to address gaps or weaknesses. This includes revising procedures, adding new controls, and improving communication protocols. Think of it as refining your emergency kit – you must ensure you're better prepared for the following incident.

3. Employee Training and Awareness: Additional training and awareness programs based on the lessons learned from the incident can help employees better recognize and respond to future threats. It's like teaching everyone in your organization to be a better digital bodyguard – the more they know, the better they can protect themselves and the organization.

4. Continuous Improvement: Continuous improvement involves regularly reviewing and updating your cybersecurity measures to ensure they remain effective. This includes conducting regular security assessments, implementing new controls, and providing ongoing training. It's like refining your skills during your adventure – the more you practice, the better you'll become.

Building Resilience

Building resilience involves preparing for the unexpected and ensuring your organization can recover quickly from cyber incidents. Here are some key strategies for building resilience:

1. Developing Robust Incident Response Plans: Developing robust incident response plans is essential for building resilience. This includes creating detailed procedures for detecting, containing, eradicating, and recovering from cyber incidents. Think of it as having a backup plan for your adventure – you must be prepared for surprises.

2. Investing in Cyber Insurance: Cyber insurance can provide your organization with extra protection. Cyber insurance is designed to cover the financial costs of cyber incidents, such as legal fees, data recovery, and business interruption. It's like having a safety net that cushions the blow when things go wrong.

3. Fostering a Culture of Cybersecurity Awareness: Fostering a culture of cybersecurity awareness ensures that everyone in the organization understands the importance of cybersecurity and takes responsibility for protecting digital assets. This includes providing regular training, promoting best practices, and encouraging employees to report potential threats. It's like having a team of vigilant guards – the more aware they are, the better they can protect the organization.

4. Collaborating with External Partners: External partners such as law enforcement, regulatory agencies, and cybersecurity experts can help enhance your organization's resilience. This includes sharing information, coordinating response efforts, and seeking expert guidance. It's like having allies in your adventure – the more support you have, the better you can handle challenges.

Conclusion

Incident response and recovery are critical components of a robust cybersecurity strategy. By preparing for cyber incidents, executing effective response plans, and learning from past incidents, CFOs can help their organizations build resilience and protect their digital assets. Building a culture of cybersecurity awareness and collaborating with external partners further reinforces these efforts, ensuring that your organization is well-equipped to tackle the digital challenges of 2025.

In conclusion, managing cyber incidents requires preparation, vigilance, and continuous improvement. By embracing their role in cybersecurity and working closely with IT and security teams, CFOs can lead their organizations to a secure and resilient future. So, put on your incident response hat and get ready to navigate the world of cybersecurity – the digital challenges of 2025 await.

Chapter 9: Cybersecurity Governance

In cybersecurity, governance is the backbone that supports all other efforts. It ensures that policies, procedures, and responsibilities are clearly defined and followed, creating a structured approach to managing cybersecurity risks. This chapter delves into establishing cybersecurity policies and procedures, defining roles and responsibilities, and building a cybersecurity culture within your organization. And, of course, we'll keep things engaging with a touch of light professional humor.

Establishing Cybersecurity Policies and Procedures

Creating robust cybersecurity policies and procedures is like laying the foundation for a sturdy house. Without a solid foundation, the entire structure is at risk. Here are some key steps for establishing effective cybersecurity policies and procedures:

1. Defining Policies: Cybersecurity policies are formal documents that outline your organization's approach to managing cybersecurity risks. These policies should cover various topics, including data protection, access controls, incident response, and employee training. Think of policies as the rulebook for your digital fortress – everyone needs to know the rules to keep things secure.

2. Developing Procedures: Procedures are detailed instructions on implementing the policies. They provide step-by-step guidance on configuring firewalls, conducting security assessments, and responding to incidents. It's like having a manual for assembling furniture – you need clear instructions to put everything together correctly.

3. Involving Stakeholders: Involving stakeholders in developing policies and procedures is essential for ensuring they are comprehensive and practical. This includes input from IT, security, legal, HR, and other relevant departments. Think of it as a team effort – everyone must contribute to build a strong foundation.

4. Regular Review and Update: Cybersecurity policies and procedures should be regularly reviewed and updated to ensure they remain practical and relevant. This includes incorporating lessons learned from incidents, addressing new threats, and complying with regulatory changes. It's like maintaining a house – you must make repairs and updates to keep it in good condition.

Defining Roles and Responsibilities

Clearly defining roles and responsibilities is crucial for effective cybersecurity governance. It ensures everyone knows their part in protecting the organization's digital assets. Here are some key considerations for defining roles and responsibilities:

1. Leadership Commitment: Leadership commitment is essential for fostering a culture of cybersecurity. Senior leaders should demonstrate their commitment by prioritizing cybersecurity, allocating resources, and leading by example. It's like having a captain who steers the ship – everyone follows their lead.

2. Assigning Responsibilities: Assigning specific responsibilities to individuals and teams ensures that tasks are clearly defined and accountability is established. This includes roles such as Chief Information Security Officer (CISO), IT security team, incident response team, and data protection officer. Think of it as assigning roles in a play – everyone needs to know their lines and cues.

3. Cross-Functional Collaboration: Effective cybersecurity requires collaboration across various departments. This includes working with IT, security, legal, HR, and other teams to implement and maintain security measures. It's like playing on a sports team – everyone must work together to succeed.

4. Employee Engagement: Engaging employees in cybersecurity efforts is essential for building a strong security culture. This includes training, promoting awareness, and encouraging employees to report potential threats. Think of it as having a team of vigilant guards – the more aware they are, the better they can protect the organization.

Building a Cybersecurity Culture

Creating a cybersecurity culture is essential for long-term success. A strong cybersecurity culture ensures that everyone in the organization understands the importance of cybersecurity and takes responsibility for protecting digital assets. Here are some strategies for building a cybersecurity culture:

1. Leadership Commitment: Leadership commitment is crucial for fostering a cybersecurity culture. When leaders prioritize cybersecurity and lead by example, it sends a clear message to the rest of the organization. It's like having a captain who steers the ship – everyone follows their lead.

2. Regular Communication: Regular communication about cybersecurity risks and best practices helps keep cybersecurity at the top of employees' minds. This can include newsletters, training sessions, and security alerts. It's like keeping everyone in the loop – the more informed they are, the better they can protect themselves and the organization.

3. Incentivizing Best Practices: Incentivizing employees to follow cybersecurity best practices can help reinforce positive behavior. This can include rewards for completing training programs, recognizing employees who identify potential threats, and incorporating cybersecurity into performance evaluations. It's like giving a gold star for good behavior – encouraging everyone to do their best.

4. Creating a Supportive Environment: Creating a supportive environment where employees feel comfortable reporting potential threats and asking questions is essential for building a cybersecurity culture. This includes providing clear channels for reporting incidents and offering employee support and resources. It's like having an open-door policy – the more approachable you are, the more likely employees will come to you with concerns.

Implementing Cybersecurity Best Practices

Implementing cybersecurity best practices is essential for building a robust defense against cyber threats. Here are some key best practices to consider:

1. Conducting Regular Security Assessments: Regular security assessments help identify vulnerabilities and ensure effective security measures. This includes vulnerability scans, penetration testing, and security audits. It's like getting a regular check-up at the doctor – you need to catch any issues early before they become serious problems.

2. Implementing Multi-Factor Authentication (MFA): MFA adds an extra layer of security by requiring users to provide multiple forms of verification before accessing systems or data. This can include something they know (e.g., a password), something they have (e.g., a smartphone), or something they are (e.g., a fingerprint). Think of MFA as the digital equivalent of a double-lock system – it's much harder to break in.

3. Encrypting Sensitive Data: Encryption is the process of converting data into a secure format that can only be accessed by authorized individuals. It ensures that sensitive information remains confidential and protected from unauthorized access. It's like putting your valuables in a safe – only those with the key can access them.

4. Providing Regular Training and Awareness Programs: Employees are often the first line of defense against cyber threats. Providing regular cybersecurity training and awareness programs can help employees recognize and respond to potential threats. It's like teaching everyone in your organization to be a digital bodyguard – the more they know, the better they can protect themselves and the organization.

5. Developing an Incident Response Plan: Despite your best efforts, cyber incidents can still occur. An incident response plan ensures you can respond quickly and effectively to minimize damage. This plan should outline the steps to take in the event of a cyber incident, including how to contain the threat, mitigate damage, and recover. Think of it as your digital fire drill – everyone must know what to do when things go wrong.

Continuous Improvement

Cybersecurity is an ongoing process that requires continuous improvement. Here are some key strategies for ensuring continuous improvement:

1. Regular Review and Update: Regularly review and update your cybersecurity policies, procedures, and controls to ensure they remain practical and relevant. This includes incorporating lessons learned from incidents, addressing new threats, and complying with regulatory changes. It's like maintaining a house – you must make repairs and updates to keep it in good condition.

2. Monitoring and Reporting: Continuous monitoring of your systems is essential for detecting potential threats and responding quickly to incidents. This includes using tools such as intrusion detection systems (IDS), security information and event management (SIEM) systems, and network monitoring tools. It's like watching the weather during your adventure – you must be prepared for changes.

3. Learning from Incidents: Conducting post-incident reviews is essential for understanding what happened, how it was handled, and what can be improved. This involves analyzing the incident, reviewing the response, and identifying areas for improvement. It's like debriefing after a mission – you need to know what went well and what didn't to improve for next time.

4. Staying Informed: Staying informed about emerging threats and trends is essential for preparing for the digital challenges of 2025. This includes monitoring industry reports, attending conferences, and participating in cybersecurity forums. It's like watching the horizon during your adventure – you must know what's coming.

Conclusion

Cybersecurity governance is the backbone of all other efforts to manage cybersecurity risks. By establishing robust policies and procedures, defining clear roles and responsibilities, and building a strong cybersecurity culture, organizations can create a structured approach to protecting their digital assets. Implementing best practices and ensuring continuous improvement further reinforce these efforts, ensuring security measures remain effective and relevant.

In conclusion, effective cybersecurity governance requires strategic planning, collaboration, and continuous improvement. By embracing their role in cybersecurity and working closely with IT and security teams, CFOs can lead their organizations to a secure and resilient future. So, put on your cybersecurity governance hat and get ready to build a strong foundation for your digital fortress – the digital challenges of 2025 await.

Chapter 10: Collaboration and Communication

In cybersecurity, collaboration and communication are the glue that holds everything together. Without them, even the best-laid plans can fall apart. This chapter delves into the essentials of working with IT and security teams, communicating cybersecurity efforts to the board and stakeholders, and engaging with external partners and regulators. And, of course, we'll keep things engaging with a touch of light professional humor.

Working with IT and Security Teams

Effective collaboration with IT and security teams is crucial for a successful cybersecurity strategy. These teams are on the front lines, implementing and maintaining security measures and responding to incidents. Here are some key techniques for working effectively with IT and security teams:

First and foremost, establish clear communication channels. Regular meetings, status updates, and open communication lines ensure everyone is on the same page. Think of it as a well-coordinated dance – everyone needs to know the steps to avoid stepping on each other's toes.

Next, define roles and responsibilities. Clearly outlining who is responsible for what helps prevent confusion and ensures that tasks are completed efficiently. It's like assigning roles in a play – everyone must know their lines and cues to deliver a stellar performance.

Encourage collaboration and teamwork. Foster a culture where IT and security teams work together to achieve common goals. This includes sharing information, resources, and expertise. Think of it as a sports team – everyone needs to work together to win the game.

Provide support and resources. Ensure that IT and security teams have the tools, training, and resources to do their jobs effectively. It's like equipping knights with the best armor and weapons – they need the right gear to protect the kingdom.

Communicating Cybersecurity Efforts to the Board and Stakeholders

Communicating cybersecurity efforts to the board and stakeholders is essential for gaining their support and ensuring cybersecurity remains a priority. Here are some key strategies for effective communication:

First, speak their language. Avoid technical jargon and use clear, concise language that the board and stakeholders can understand. It's like translating a foreign language – ensuring your message is clear and accessible.

Next, focus on the business impact. Highlight how cybersecurity efforts align with the organization's goals and objectives. Emphasize the potential risks and benefits regarding financial impact, reputation, and regulatory compliance. Think of it as making a business case – you must show how cybersecurity contributes to the bottom line.

Provide regular updates. Keep the board and stakeholders informed about cybersecurity initiatives, progress, and challenges. This includes providing regular reports, presentations, and briefings. It's like keeping everyone in the loop – the more informed they are, the better they can support your efforts.

Use metrics and data. Use metrics and data to demonstrate the effectiveness of cybersecurity measures and the progress being made. This includes key performance indicators (KPIs), benchmarks, and trends. Think of it as showing your work – you must provide evidence to support your claims.

Engaging with External Partners and Regulators

Engaging with external partners and regulators is essential to staying compliant with regulations, sharing information, and enhancing your cybersecurity efforts. Here are some key strategies for effective engagement:

First, build relationships. Establish relationships with external partners, such as law enforcement, regulatory agencies, and industry groups. This includes attending conferences, participating in forums, and networking. It's like making friends – the more connections you have, the better.

Next, share information. This includes sharing information about threats, vulnerabilities, and best practices with external partners, participating in information-sharing initiatives, and collaborating on joint efforts. Think of it as being a good neighbor – sharing information helps everyone stay safe.

Stay compliant. Ensure that your organization complies with relevant regulations and standards. This includes staying informed about regulatory changes, conducting regular audits, and addressing compliance gaps. It's like following the rules; you need to keep on the right side of the law.

Seek guidance and support. Don't be afraid to seek guidance and support from external partners and regulators. This includes asking for advice, attending training sessions, and leveraging their expertise. Consider asking for directions – sometimes you need help finding your way.

Building a Culture of Collaboration and Communication

Creating a culture of collaboration and communication is essential for long-term success. A strong culture ensures everyone understands the importance of working together and communicating effectively. Here are some strategies for building a culture of collaboration and communication:

First, lead by example. Leadership commitment is crucial for fostering a culture of collaboration and communication. When leaders prioritize these values and lead by example, it sends a clear message to the rest of the organization. It's like having a captain who steers the ship – everyone follows their lead.

Next, provide training and resources. Provide training and resources to help employees develop their collaboration and communication skills. This includes workshops, seminars, and online courses. Think of it as giving everyone a toolkit – the more tools they have, the better they can work together.

Encourage open communication. Create an environment where employees feel comfortable sharing ideas, asking questions, and providing feedback. This includes establishing open-door policies, holding regular meetings, and promoting transparency. It's like having an open forum – the more voices you hear, the better.

Recognize and reward collaboration. Recognize and reward employees who demonstrate strong collaboration and communication skills. This can include awards, bonuses, and public recognition. Think of it as giving a gold star for good behavior – encouraging everyone to do their best.

Leveraging Technology for Collaboration and Communication

Technology plays a crucial role in facilitating collaboration and communication. Here are some key technologies to consider:

First, collaboration tools. Collaboration tools like project management software, team messaging apps, and document-sharing platforms help teams work together more effectively. It's like having a virtual office – everyone can collaborate, no matter where they are.

Next, video conferencing. Video conferencing tools enable face-to-face communication, even when team members are in different locations. This helps build relationships and fosters a sense of connection. Think of it as a virtual meeting room – you can see and hear everyone, just like in person.

Security information and event management (SIEM) systems help organizations monitor and analyze security events in real-time. This enables teams to detect and respond to threats more quickly and effectively. It's like having a security camera; you can see what's happening and take action when needed.

Incident response platforms help teams manage and coordinate their response to cyber incidents. This includes tracking incidents, assigning tasks, and documenting actions. Think of it as a command center; everyone knows their role and can work together to resolve the incident.

Conclusion

Collaboration and communication are essential components of a robust cybersecurity strategy. By working effectively with IT and security teams, communicating cybersecurity efforts to the board and stakeholders, and engaging with external partners and regulators, organizations can build a strong defense against cyber threats. Building a culture of collaboration and communication further reinforces these efforts, ensuring that everyone in the organization understands the importance of working together and communicating effectively.

In conclusion, effective collaboration and communication require a combination of strategic planning, leadership commitment, and continuous improvement. By embracing their role in cybersecurity and working closely with IT and security teams, CFOs can lead their organizations to a secure and resilient future. So, put on your collaboration and communication hat and get ready to build strong relationships – the digital challenges of 2025 await.

Chapter 11: Future Trends in Cybersecurity

As we look ahead, the cybersecurity landscape continues to evolve rapidly. New technologies, emerging threats, and changing regulations shape how organizations approach cybersecurity. In this chapter, we'll explore some of the key trends expected to impact cybersecurity in the coming years and how working with a Managed Service Provider (MSP) can help organizations stay ahead of the curve. And, of course, we'll keep things engaging with a touch of light professional humor.

Predicting Future Cyber Threats

The world of cyber threats is constantly changing, with new and more sophisticated attacks always emerging. Here are some of the key trends in future cyber threats:

1. AI-Powered Attacks: As artificial intelligence (AI) continues to advance, cybercriminals are leveraging AI to enhance their attack strategies. AI-powered attacks can adapt and learn from defenses, making them more challenging to detect and counter. It's like facing an opponent who gets smarter with every move you make – a digital game of chess where the stakes are high.

2. Ransomware Evolution: Ransomware attacks have become increasingly prevalent and sophisticated. In the future, we can expect to see more targeted attacks, with cybercriminals focusing on high-value targets and demanding larger ransoms. It's like a digital version of a heist movie, except the bad guys are after your data instead of your diamonds.

3. IoT Vulnerabilities: The Internet of Things (IoT) has brought convenience and connectivity to our lives but has also introduced new security risks. IoT devices, from smart thermostats to connected cars, can be exploited by cybercriminals to gain access to networks. It's as if every smart device in your home has the potential to become a spy – a digital version of "Big Brother."

4. Supply Chain Attacks: Cybercriminals increasingly target supply chains to infiltrate organizations. They can gain access to the primary target by compromising a supplier or vendor. It's like sneaking into a castle by hiding in a delivery truck – a clever but dangerous tactic.

5. Quantum Computing Threats: Quantum computing promises to revolutionize technology but poses a significant threat to cybersecurity. Quantum computers can potentially break encryption methods that are currently considered secure. It's like discovering that the lock on your front door can be picked with a paperclip – a game-changer.

Innovations in Cybersecurity Technologies

As cyber threats evolve, so do the technologies designed to combat them. Here are some of the key innovations in cybersecurity technologies that are expected to shape the future:

1. AI and Machine Learning: AI and machine learning are transforming the cybersecurity landscape by enhancing the ability to detect and respond to threats. These technologies can analyze vast amounts of data to identify patterns and anomalies, making them more effective at detecting and mitigating threats. It's like having a super-smart detective on your team – they can spot clues that others might miss.

2. Zero Trust Architecture: Zero Trust is a security model that assumes that no one can be trusted by default, whether inside or outside the network. It requires strict verification for every user and device attempting to access resources. Consider it a digital version of "trust but verify" – a cautious but practical approach.

3. Extended Detection and Response (XDR): XDR is an integrated threat detection approach that combines data from multiple security tools and sources. It provides a holistic view of the security landscape, enabling faster and more effective threat detection and response. It's like having a bird's-eye view of the battlefield – you can see the whole picture and respond accordingly.

4. Secure Access Service Edge (SASE): SASE is a cloud-based security model that combines network security and wide-area networking (WAN) capabilities. It provides secure access to resources regardless of location, making it ideal for remote work environments. Think of it as a digital fortress in the cloud – safe and accessible from anywhere.

5. Blockchain Security: Blockchain technology, known for its use in cryptocurrencies, is being explored for its potential to enhance cybersecurity. Its decentralized and immutable nature makes it difficult for cybercriminals to tamper with data. It's like having a digital ledger that can't be altered – a secure and transparent way to protect information.

Preparing for the Future: Continuous Improvement

As the cybersecurity landscape evolves, organizations must proactively prepare for future challenges. Here are some key strategies for continuous improvement:

1. Staying Informed: Staying informed about emerging threats and trends is essential for preparing for the future. This includes monitoring industry reports, attending conferences, and participating in cybersecurity forums. It's like watching the horizon during your adventure – you must know what's coming.

2. Adopting New Technologies: Adopting new technologies can help organizations stay ahead of the curve and enhance their cybersecurity efforts. This includes leveraging AI, machine learning, and automation to improve security measures. It's like upgrading your gear for the adventure – the better equipped you are, the more successful you'll be.

3. Continuous Training and Awareness: Regular training and awareness programs ensure that employees are up-to-date with the latest cybersecurity practices. This includes training on new technologies, emerging threats, and best practices. It's like teaching everyone in your organization to be a better digital bodyguard; the more they know, the better they can protect themselves and the organization.

4. Regular Security Assessments: Conducting regular security assessments helps identify vulnerabilities and ensure that security measures are effective. This includes vulnerability scans, penetration testing, and security audits. It's like getting a regular check-up at the doctor – you need to catch any issues early before they become serious problems.

5. Building Resilience: Building resilience involves preparing for the unexpected and ensuring your organization can recover quickly from cyber incidents. This includes developing robust incident response plans, investing in cyber insurance, and fostering a culture of cybersecurity awareness. It's like having a backup plan for your adventure – you must be prepared for surprises.

How Working with an MSP Can Help

Managed Service Providers (MSPs) play a crucial role in helping organizations navigate the future of cybersecurity. Here are some ways that working with an MSP can help:

1. Access to Expertise: MSPs offer specialized skills and knowledge, allowing organizations to benefit from their expertise without having to hire additional staff. It's like having a team of experts on call; you can tap into their knowledge whenever you need it.

2. Staying Informed: MSPs stay up-to-date with cybersecurity trends, threats, and technologies. They can provide valuable insights and recommendations to help organizations stay ahead of the curve. It's like having a personal advisor who informs you about the latest developments.

3. Enhancing Incident Response: MSPs can enhance an organization's incident response capabilities by providing expert guidance and support during cyber incidents. They can help respond quickly and effectively, minimizing damage and ensuring a swift recovery. Think of them as digital first responders – they quickly contain the threat and mitigate damage.

4. Improving Compliance: MSPs can help organizations navigate the complex landscape of cybersecurity regulations and compliance requirements. They can assist with meeting standards such as GDPR, HIPAA, and PCI DSS, ensuring that organizations stay compliant. It's like having a legal advisor who keeps you out of trouble.

5. Optimizing Security Investments: MSPs can help organizations optimize their security investments by providing insights into the most effective and cost-efficient security measures. They can recommend technologies and solutions that align with the organization's needs and budget. It's like having a financial advisor who helps you make smart investments.

Conclusion

The future of cybersecurity is filled with challenges and opportunities. By staying informed about emerging threats and trends, adopting new technologies, and continuously improving security measures, organizations can build a robust defense against cyber threats. Working with an MSP can further enhance these efforts, providing access to expertise, improving incident response, and ensuring compliance with regulations.

In conclusion, preparing for the future of cybersecurity requires a combination of strategic planning, continuous improvement, and collaboration with experts. By embracing their role in cybersecurity and working closely with MSPs, CFOs can lead their organizations to a secure and resilient future. So, put on your future trends hat and get ready to navigate the ever-changing landscape of cybersecurity – the digital challenges of 2025 and beyond await.

Chapter 12: Conclusion

As we reach the end of our journey through the "CFO's Handbook to Cyber Security 2025 Edition," it's time to reflect on the key takeaways and the ongoing role of the CFO in cybersecurity. This chapter will recap the essential points covered in the book, emphasize the importance of continuous improvement, and highlight the CFO's strategic role in ensuring the organization's security. And, of course, we'll keep things engaging with a touch of light professional humor.

Recap of Key Takeaways

Throughout this book, we've explored various aspects of cybersecurity, from understanding cyber threats to building a robust cybersecurity strategy. Let's take a moment to recap some of the key takeaways:

First and foremost, the evolving role of the CFO in cybersecurity cannot be overstated. CFOs are not just financial stewards but strategic leaders driving cybersecurity initiatives. Their financial expertise allows them to allocate resources effectively, ensuring that cybersecurity measures are robust and cost-efficient. It's like having a superhero who can balance the books and fend off cyber villains – a true multitasker.

Understanding cyber threats is crucial for effective cybersecurity. From malware and phishing to advanced persistent threats (APTs) and ransomware, CFOs must be aware of the various threats that can impact their organization. It's like knowing the enemy – you must understand their tactics to defend against them.

Cybersecurity frameworks and standards provide a structured approach to managing cybersecurity risks. Frameworks such as NIST, ISO/IEC 27001, and CIS Controls offer valuable guidance for implementing best practices and ensuring compliance with regulatory requirements. Think of them as the blueprints for building a secure digital fortress – follow the plans, and you'll be in good shape.

Risk management and assessment are critical components of a robust cybersecurity strategy. By identifying and assessing cyber risks, implementing risk mitigation strategies, and understanding the role of cyber insurance, CFOs can help their organizations build a strong defense against cyber threats. It's like preparing for a grand adventure – you must know the terrain and pack the right gear.

Building a cybersecurity strategy involves developing a comprehensive plan, aligning it with business objectives, budgeting effectively, and preparing for emerging threats. Collaboration with IT and security teams, clear communication, and continuous improvement are essential for success. It's like planning a journey – you need a roadmap, the right team, and the flexibility to adapt to changing conditions.

Technology and tools play a crucial role in enhancing cybersecurity efforts. Organizations have various options to protect their digital assets, from firewalls and intrusion detection systems (IDS) to AI and automation. Choosing the right cybersecurity vendors and working with Managed Service Providers (MSPs) can further strengthen defenses. It's like having a well-stocked toolbox – you need the right tools for the job.

Incident response and recovery are essential for minimizing damage and recovering quickly from cyber incidents. Developing robust incident response plans, conducting post-incident reviews and building resilience are key strategies for effective incident management. It's like having an emergency kit – you need to know what to do when things go wrong.

Cybersecurity governance ensures that policies, procedures, and responsibilities are clearly defined and followed. Building a strong cybersecurity culture, implementing best practices, and providing continuous improvement are essential for long-term success. It's like laying the foundation for a sturdy house – without a solid foundation, the entire structure is at risk.

Collaboration and communication are vital for a successful cybersecurity strategy. Working with IT and security teams, communicating cybersecurity efforts to the board and stakeholders, and engaging with external partners and regulators are key strategies for building strong relationships and enhancing security efforts. It's like having a well-coordinated dance – everyone needs to know the steps to avoid stepping on each other's toes.

Future trends in cybersecurity, such as AI-powered attacks, ransomware evolution, IoT vulnerabilities, and quantum computing threats, require organizations to stay informed and proactive. Adopting new technologies, continuous training and awareness, regular security assessments, and building resilience are essential for preparing for the digital challenges 2026 and beyond. It's like keeping an eye on the horizon – you must know what's coming to stay ahead of the curve.

The CFO's Ongoing Role in Cybersecurity

As we look to the future, the role of the CFO in cybersecurity will continue to evolve. CFOs must embrace their strategic role and proactively protect their organizations. Here are some key aspects of the CFO's ongoing role in cybersecurity:

First, leadership commitment is crucial. CFOs must demonstrate their commitment to cybersecurity by prioritizing it as a key component of their strategic planning. This includes allocating resources, leading by example, and fostering a culture of cybersecurity awareness. It's like being the captain of a ship – everyone looks to the captain for guidance and direction.

Next, collaboration and teamwork are essential. CFOs must work closely with IT and security teams, the board, stakeholders, and external partners to implement and maintain security measures. This includes sharing information, coordinating efforts, and leveraging expertise. Think of it as playing on a sports team – everyone must work together to succeed.

Continuous improvement is key to staying ahead of emerging threats. CFOs must regularly review and update cybersecurity measures, conduct security assessments, and provide ongoing training and awareness programs. It's like refining your skills – the more you practice, the better you'll become.

Staying informed about emerging threats and trends is essential for proactive cybersecurity. CFOs must monitor industry reports, attend conferences, and participate in cybersecurity forums to stay up-to-date with the latest developments. It's like keeping an eye on the horizon – you must know what's coming to stay ahead of the curve.

Building resilience involves preparing for the unexpected and ensuring the organization can recover quickly from cyber incidents. CFOs must develop robust incident response plans, invest in cyber insurance, and foster a culture of cybersecurity awareness. It's like having a backup plan – you must be prepared for surprises.

Conclusion

In conclusion, the "CFO's Handbook to Cyber Security 2025 Edition" has provided valuable insights into the CFO's evolving role in cybersecurity, the importance of understanding cyber threats, building a robust cybersecurity strategy, leveraging technology and tools, and preparing for future challenges. By embracing their role in cybersecurity and working closely with IT and security teams, the board, stakeholders, and external partners, CFOs can lead their organizations to a secure and resilient future.

As we navigate the digital challenges of 2025 and beyond, staying informed, proactive, and committed to continuous improvement is essential. Cybersecurity is an ongoing journey that requires vigilance, collaboration, and adaptability. So, put on your cybersecurity hat, gather your team, and get ready to tackle the ever-changing landscape of cybersecurity – the adventure awaits.

Thank you for joining us on this journey through the "CFO's Handbook to Cyber Security 2025 Edition." We hope this book's insights and strategies will help you build a strong defense against cyber threats and lead your organization to a secure and resilient future. Remember, the role of the CFO in cybersecurity is not just a responsibility – it's an opportunity to make a lasting impact and protect the digital assets that drive your organization's success.

I will end this handbook with a quote inspired to make you think about the limitless boundaries that exist in worlds both real and imagined.

"I'm going to show them a world without you. A world without rules and controls, without borders or boundaries. A world where anything is possible. Where we go from there is a choice I leave to you."

-   *Neo, The Matrix (1999)*

www.ingramcontent.com/pod-product-compliance
Lightning Source LLC
LaVergne TN
LVHW051618050326
832903LV00033B/4550